Netball

Contents

When using this book, concentrate on one coaching point at a time. Practise each point u… mastered it before moving on to the next one. You do not ne… cover. Choose a skill you want t… with the outcome.

Although the … nder bias is intended.

INTRODUCTION

Netball is a dynamic, fast, stop-start sport which involves players jumping, landing, throwing, catching and shooting the ball in lots of different ways and from lots of different positions.

SCORING

To win a game of netball a team must score more goals than their opponents. While one team is trying to keep possession and score off it, the other team is trying to deny their opponents space and chances to score. They are also trying to win the ball back, either through intercepting it, or by causing the other team to make an error.

The way in which a team does this comes down to each individual's skill level and their ability to apply it to the game.

WHAT MAKES A GOOD NETBALLER?

- Sound decision making
- Good individual ball skills
- Ability to read the game
- Speed and power
- Quick reactions and agility
- Good vision
- Confidence
- Ability to thrive under pressure

INTERNATIONAL NETBALL

In international netball, different countries play in contrasting styles. For example, Australia, one of the world's best teams, are renowned for their tight one-on-one marking and hard, flat, precision passing. New Zealand, currently ranked number two, mark less tightly and like to release the ball into space when attacking. Malawi are becoming known for their flamboyant, creative and rapid netball, which can result in a lot of passes in order to retain possession.

DID YOU KNOW?

The highest score in international netball was 116-26 when New Zealand defeated Sri Lanka in 2002. This was also the biggest margin recorded.
The lowest score was 17-85, when Malaysia lost to Australia in 1998.

IMPROVING SKILLS

There are many skills that are applicable to all positions in netball, however some positions require specific skills which should be practised daily if you want to be really good.

This book is intended to help you to improve your basic skills and inspire you to challenge yourself to be the best that you can be.

Netball requires lots of different skills, but the object of the game is to score as many goals as possible.

COURT AND **POSITIONS**

There are seven players in a netball team, and a full game lasts for an hour. If you are at primary school, you may play a shorter version of the game called High Five. The rules are slightly different, but the skills needed are just the same.

COURT LAYOUT

The court is laid out as shown in the diagram below. It is 30.5 metres long (100 feet) and 15.25 metres (50 feet) wide. It is divided into three sections by two transverse lines. A centre circle 90 cm (3 feet) wide is located in the middle of the court.

At each end of the court there is a 4.9-metre-wide (16-feet-wide) semi-circular shooting circle, known as the goal circle, and all shots at goal must be taken from inside it.

The goal posts are 3.05 metres (10 feet) high from the top of the ring to the ground and, unlike basketball, they have no backboards.

The markings and layout of a netball court.

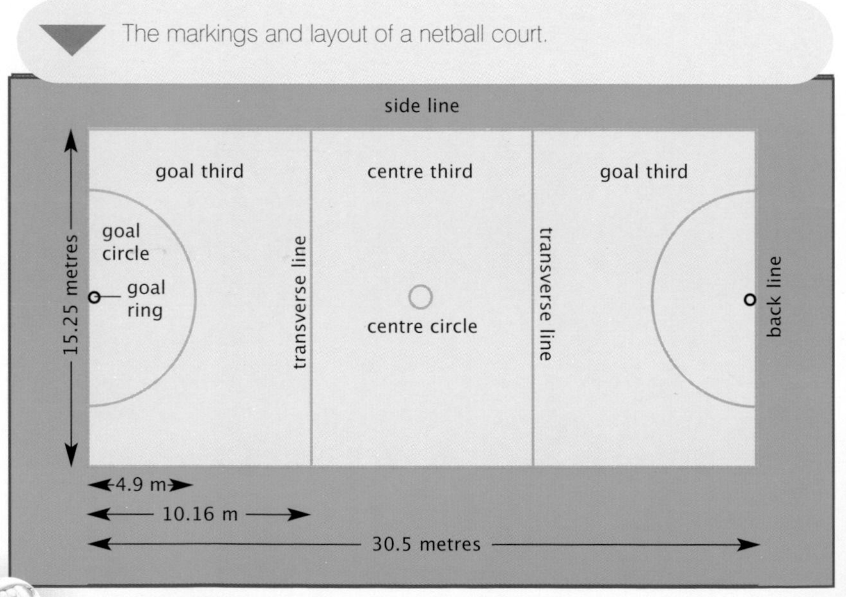

POSITIONS

Including substitutes, there are twelve players in a full netball team, although only seven are on court at any one time. These seven players are given named positions. Each position is only allowed in certain areas of the court (marked 1 to 5 on the diagram on page 6): if a player crosses over into a section of the court that is not part of her playing area she is deemed 'offside'. Each player's role is:

The Centre starts the game.

Goal shooter (GS)

To score goals and work with the GA.

Goal attack (GA)

To score goals and feed the GS.

Wing attack (WA)

To feed the ball to the GA and GK.

Centre (C)

To start the game (take the centre pass) and link the defence and attack.

Wing defence (WD)

To try to intercept the ball and get it to a member of her own team. To try to prevent the WA of the opposite team from feeding the GA or GK of her team.

Goal defence (GD)

To try to intercept the ball and reduce the effectiveness of the other team's GA.

Goal keeper (GK)

To work with the GD and try to stop the other team's GS from scoring goals.

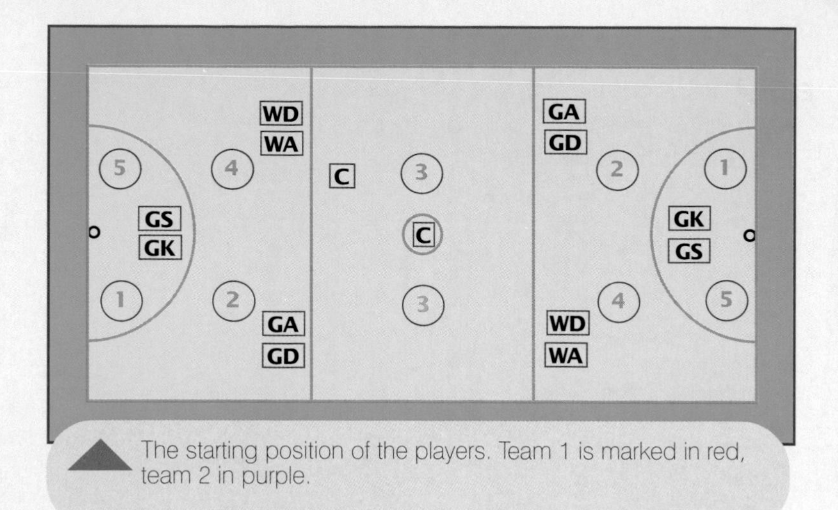

The starting position of the players. Team 1 is marked in red, team 2 in purple.

PLAYING THE GAME

A netball game is divided into four 15-minute quarters. There is a half-time interval of five to ten minutes, while the intervals between the first and second quarters, and the third and fourth quarters, are three minutes long.

The object of the game is to score more goals than the opposing team. A goal is scored when the ball passes over and completely through the goal ring.

DID YOU KNOW?

The highest goal scorer in an international match is Irene van Dyk of New Zealand, who scored 58 from 62 attempts (94 per cent) against Sri Lanka in 2002.

Lining up

At the beginning of each quarter, the two teams must position themselves on the court. The usual starting positions are shown on the diagram above, although the rules only require GA, GD, WA and WD to be in the goal third areas of the court (areas 1, 2, 4 and 5). Only the two centres are allowed in the centre third (area 3).The centre with the ball must be completely in the centre circle. The other centre is allowed anywhere in the centre third.

PLAYER MOVEMENTS

Each player is only allowed in certain areas of the court. These areas are marked on the diagram opposite as numbers in circles. The colour of each circle applies to the team of the same colour.

Abbreviation	Position	Areas allowed
GS	Goal shooter	1 and 2
GA	Goal attack	1, 2 and 3
WA	Wing attack	2 and 3
C	Centre	2, 3 and 4
WD	Wing defence	3 and 4
GD	Goal defence	3, 4 and 5
GK	Goal keeper	4 and 5

Centre pass

When the whistle blows and the game starts the Centre has to pass the ball within three seconds. The player catching the ball must have at least one foot in the centre third to receive the ball. This means that when the whistle blows there is a lot of movement on a netball court!

Game play

Starting from the centre pass, a team will try to pass the ball between players until it reaches the goal circle and a player can attempt a shot at goal. Meanwhile, the opposing team will try to intercept the ball and get it to the other end of the court in order for their team to score goals instead.

Goal scoring

Only GS and GA can score, and they must be completely within the goal circle to try for goal. When a goal has been scored, all the players resume their starting positions and the process starts all over again.

RULES OF THE GAME

Netball is a non-contact sport, which means you must not touch an opponent on purpose. Here are some of the rules you will need to understand before you play.

REPLAY/ REPOSSESSION

When you catch the ball, you are not allowed to bat it, dribble it or lose control and then regain it. These are considered infringements of the rules.

THREE SECONDS

Once in possession of the ball you have three seconds to make a pass. If you take longer, possession is awarded to the other team.

FOOTWORK

When you catch the ball, try and land one-two with your feet, or receive the pass with only one foot on the ground (the landing foot). You can then choose to step with the other foot, while lifting your landing foot, and throw the ball before you put your landing foot back on the ground. Or you can pivot on your landing foot and move the other foot any number of times (within the three seconds). But you cannot re-ground, move or hop on the landing foot until you have thrown the ball, otherwise it is an offence known as stepping.

DEFENCE

When an opponent is in possession of the ball you have to be at least 90 cm (3 feet) away from her (the distance of the centre circle). You cannot knock the ball out of your opponent's hands, but you can win the ball once she has passed it.

When your opponent is not in possession of the ball, you can be as close to her as you wish without making contact.

If you make contact with an opposing player, or if you touch the ball when it is being held by an opponent, a penalty pass will be awarded against you.

base, with your feet shoulder width apart, slightly flexed knees, and body upright. Practise this stance before you start. When you jump for the ball, drive your arms up to meet it.

- Next, the feeder should pass the ball so that the worker has to stretch to receive it (we call this 'on extension'). The feeder can pass it 'anywhere' – remember, variation and not passing in a pattern is key.
- The worker needs to catch using one and two hands in all positions. Sometimes you should pull the ball in close to your body before passing it back, and sometimes, if you have control, you can pass it back from the point at which you caught it.

Practise receiving the ball 'on extension'. You will need to use your fingers to pull the ball in to your body.

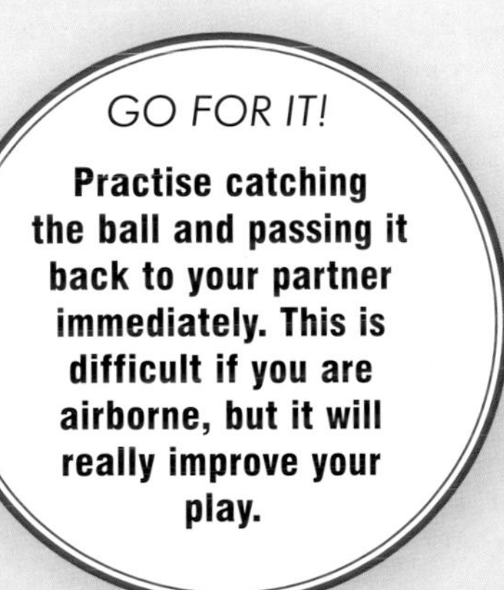

GO FOR IT!

Practise catching the ball and passing it back to your partner immediately. This is difficult if you are airborne, but it will really improve your play.

For one player

Here are a series of exercises you can try on your own. Stand about 90 cm (3 feet) in front of a wall.

- **Double hand jump taps:** You need a balanced base, feet shoulder width apart, slightly flexed knees, body upright and arms bent, with your hands 'ready' in front of and above your head.

  Push the ball against the wall about two feet above your start position. Once the ball has left your hands, jump to catch it at its highest point off the wall.

DID YOU KNOW?

Netball was first played in England in 1895. The first World Championship tournament was held in Eastbourne, Sussex, in 1963.

Land on both feet, shoulder width apart with bent knees.

- **Single hand jump taps:** As the double hand jump tap, but using only one hand.
- **Alternate hand jump taps:** Using one hand for one catch, then the other hand for the next catch.
- **Angle running takes:** Pass the ball into the wall at an angle and try and catch it on extension, running to the pass. If you pass the ball 'up and under' it will come back off the wall high, challenging you to jump for it. Experiment with the different angles and positions from which you throw the ball at the wall so that you vary the catches. Practise catching with one and two hands.

PASSING

Passing is one of the most important skills in netball. If you want to be a good player you need to be able to pass accurately.

One of the most important rules about passing is that you only have three seconds to pass the ball after you have caught it. Once you have mastered the skills you need to release the ball well, you can keep your opponents guessing by varying the timing of your release.

Chest pass

The chest pass is one of the fastest ways to get the ball from player to player. Often players have to adapt it slightly to one side or the other in order to get the ball around a defender. However, its advantage is that it is a quick pass, as the holding position and the release position are so close together.

- Start by holding the ball close to your chest in both hands with your fingers either side of the ball and your thumbs at the back (creating a 'W' shape).
- Take a step forward so that the ball moves forward as your body weight transfers. The elbows, which started comfortably by your side, straighten and your fingers and thumbs finish off pushing the ball in the direction you want it to go.

Chest pass: Hold the ball with your fingers and thumbs creating a 'W' shape.

Hold the ball close to your chest.

Take a step forward and push the ball out.

The shoulder pass: 1. Create a right angle with your throwing arm. 2. Step forward with your opposite foot and pass the ball.

Shoulder pass

The shoulder pass is the most effective for delivering a long accurate pass or for stepping around a defender and trying to get the ball away without any interference.

- Start as you would for the chest pass, holding the ball with both hands in front of you. Lift the ball to a position which creates a right angle with your shoulder, elbow and hand (one hand behind the ball). Use your right shoulder if you are right-handed, left if you are left-handed.
- Step forward with your opposite foot. As you do so, your weight is transferred forward to allow you to get power behind your pass. Extend your elbow and hand to point them in the direction you want the ball to travel, to ensure that it travels straight and flat.

Bounce pass

Most defenders hate the bounce pass! Although it is usually a slower pass than the other two, it is one which also allows the passer to 'lead' the attacker into space.

The bounce pass: 1. The ball is released close to your hip. Point your fingers in the direction you want the ball to go.
2. Step forward and thrust the ball to the ground to make the pass.

- It can be delivered from one or two hands, either from the same start position as the chest pass (though the follow-through finishes off travelling downwards), or the ball might be taken to the side of the body, similar to the shoulder pass.
- The point at which you release the pass will be dictated by the position of the defender and the place you want to pass to.
- As a general rule, the bounce pass is released close to your hip, with your hands and fingers pointing in the direction that you want the ball to travel.
- As for the chest and shoulder passes, step forward to transfer your weight and get more power behind the ball. Aim to bounce the ball about three-quarters of the way to the receiver (or even closer) to ensure that the ball bounces up between the height of the top of her legs and her waist.
- Sometimes you will want the ball to 'sit' up for the player to catch it. At other times you will keep the ball lower to make it harder for the defender to intercept.

MOVEMENT

As the ball moves down the court, a player needs to prepare to either receive it or defend it. When your team has possession of the ball, each team member needs to work hard to bring the ball down the court to the shooters so that they can score.

If you don't have possession, players need to move into positions in which they can defend against their opponent to either deny them space, force them to make errors or intercept the ball.

The best netballers have excellent movement, good agility and sound footwork. They are able to change direction, jump off one or both feet, run to receive a pass or intercept a pass to an opponent and, at the end of it all, have the control to land and stay within the rules of the game.

DID YOU KNOW?

An American woman called Clara Gregory Baer is credited with inventing netball, which developed from basketball. It is particularly popular in Australia and New Zealand as well as the West Indies, Sri Lanka and the United Kingdom, and is now played in more than 70 countries worldwide.

FOOTWORK

Speed of foot movement is very important in top-level netball. International teams incorporate speed and agility sessions within their training in order to ensure that their players get themselves in the right place at the right time. Good fitness levels are also important to ensure that the quality of their footwork doesn't deteriorate during the game as they become tired.

As we discussed earlier, when you catch the ball you want to try and land 'one-two' with your feet, or receive the pass with only one foot on the ground ('the landing

foot'). You can then choose to step with the other foot, while lifting the landing foot and throwing the ball before you re-ground the landing foot; or you can pivot on your landing foot.

Before you get in a position to catch the ball you must first make a powerful run to it. It may only involve a couple of strides, or a change of direction, but you need to start from a balanced position with your weight over your feet, knees slightly flexed, with your arms and legs ready to drive towards the ball. You need to try and reach top speed in your first few strides in order to beat a defender.

Good footwork: Always try to land with one foot first, then the other – the 'one-two' concept.

JUMPING AND LANDING

When you are jumping to catch the ball, keep your eyes on it. You can jump from one or both feet to receive the ball from your teammate with either one or two hands, or if you are trying to intercept the ball from the opposition.

When you are preparing to jump you must have your feet shoulder width apart and, as you bend your knees and generate force from the ground, drive your arms up to maximise your jump.

Make yourself as tall as possible when you jump to gain enough height to catch the ball.

To regain your balance on landing, bend your knees. Try and catch the ball as we described on page 10. Bring your arms back into your body so that you absorb the force of the pass.

PRACTICE

For one player

- While warming up, practise your footwork, jumping and landing.
- Start jogging around the court. Occasionally either toss the ball up to yourself or to your partner, or bounce the ball into the ground and then try to catch it at its highest point. Once you've caught the ball, practise landing either one-two, or on both feet at the same time.

For two players

Practise as a pair, with one ball.

- One of you is the worker and the other the feeder. Stand three feet away from each other.
- The feeder needs to pass the ball so that the worker has to jump straight up and catch it at its highest point. The worker is trying to jump straight up

DID YOU KNOW?

When netball was first played in England in 1895, the rules were so loose that teams often had different numbers of players. Also, the nets were closed at one end, meaning the umpire had to climb up to retrieve the ball from the net whenever a goal was scored!

like an arrow rather than folding in from her middle like a banana!

- When you've managed to master jumping straight, catching the ball and landing in a balanced manner, test yourself by getting your partner to throw the ball anywhere in a small area. Now you will have to work your feet to get under the ball to catch it at its highest point.

GO FOR IT!

Try to catch the ball in the air and pass it back accurately to your partner before you land.

PIVOTING

Once you've learnt how to land according to the footwork rule, you can learn how to pivot. Being able to pivot will help you to make better decisions on court by allowing you to move freely and see all your options. After jumping to receive the ball, land one-two. Ensure that you are balanced before you attempt to pivot.

Stand with your knees slightly bent and your feet shoulder width apart. Once you have decided which direction to turn, pivot on the ball of your first landing foot, using your other foot to move you around. You can move or step with your second foot as many times as needed as long as you

▲ Pivoting allows you to turn quickly and pass the ball in any direction.

don't lift up your landing foot and then put it down again. While you are pivoting keep the ball close to your body and keep your body upright. When you have chosen your passing option, make sure you have turned fully around and are facing the player you want to pass to.

PRACTICE

This is an extension of the jumping and landing practice on page 20.

- This time, as you land one-two, pivot right round on the ball of your first landing foot, so that you can see all your teammates on the court (see photos opposite).

DID YOU KNOW?

The Netball World Championships take place every four years and have been dominated by Australia. Netball was recognised as an official Olympic sport in 1995, but it is yet to be included in an Olympic Games.

Make it harder

Work in a pair, jogging around the court.

- Player one completes the practice above then passes the ball to player two.
- Player one should carry on jogging once she has passed the ball.
- Player two should catch the ball while jogging.
- Player two then lands, pivots and passes the ball back to player one.
- Keep it going as long as you can.

In threes, with two feeders, one worker and one ball.

- The two feeders stand facing each other about 10 feet apart, with the worker in between them.
- Run towards the first feeder, receive a straight line pass, land one-two, pivot and then pass to the other feeder.
- Repeat in the other direction.

Pivot practice: Without moving your first (landing) foot, use your second foot to pivot around in a 360-degree circle. The more you practise this move and the quicker you become, the more passing options you will have in a real game.

DEFENCE

When you are defending you are constantly trying to pressure your opponent into making a mistake, either through a passing or footwork error, or by anticipating when your opponent is going to pass the ball and intercepting it. A good defender needs to:

- Be quick on her feet, either to get around a player to try to intercept the ball without making contact, or to be able to recover quickly.
- Have good anticipation skills.
- Be able to read the game well.
- Deny their opposition space by using her own body within the rules of the game.
- Communicate well with her teammates.

PHASES OF DEFENCE

Coaches usually talk about defence in phases:

1. Restricting the player.
2. Going for the intercept.
3. Marking the pass and/or the shot.

Restricting the player

You can deny the opposition space by marking from the side, in front (on an angle) or from behind. In each case set up with your feet shoulder width apart, and your weight on the balls of your feet so that you are ready to move.

The defender can direct her opponent either towards a teammate, close towards a side or back line, or drive her to run tight to the ball carrier, denying the opposition a chance to gain ground.

If you are side marking, try to be 'ball side', putting yourself between the attacker and ball carrier, so that the ball has to travel over you in order to get to the attacker.

To ensure that you can see your opponent, the ball and preferably your fellow defenders, angle your body to give you a good field of vision. As the attacker moves, try to keep your start position. If you are having to look over your shoulder you need to move your feet more. Keep your head still.

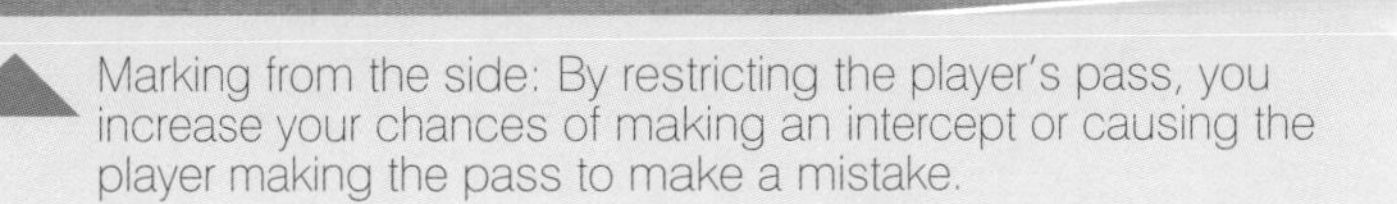

Marking from the side: By restricting the player's pass, you increase your chances of making an intercept or causing the player making the pass to make a mistake.

PRACTICE

You need one attacker and one defender.

- Mark out a box area, 3 metres by 3 metres (10 by 10 feet), using cones or jumpers.
- The aim of the practice is for the attacker to try to run to the corners three times in, say, 30 seconds. The defender has to stop her getting to the cones by staying as close to the attacker as possible and using her body angles to restrict where the attacker can go.
- Once the attacker hits one corner she can't hit it again until she goes to another corner.
- Take turns to be the attacker and the defender.

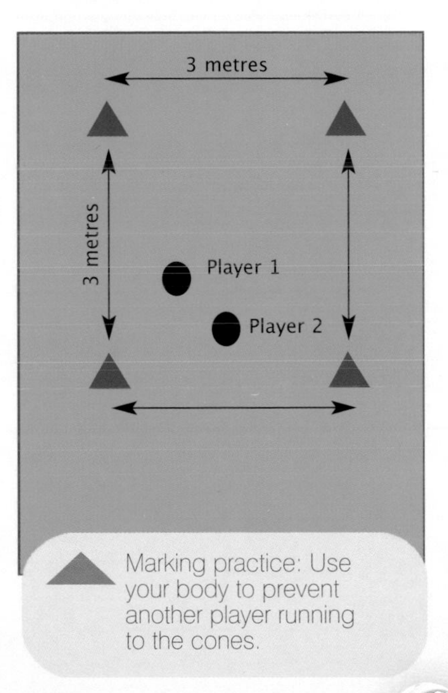

Marking practice: Use your body to prevent another player running to the cones.

Going for the intercept: Try to position yourself so that you can catch the ball as it is passed to your opponent.

Going for the intercept

Once the defender has worked on denying the attackers space, she should then try to intercept the ball.

Timing is the key. Try to anticipate when the attackers are going to release the ball, and only then commit to going for the interception. If you commit too early the ball carrier will change her mind, or the opponent you were marking may move somewhere else.

The defender should try to take the interception away from the receiver to minimise the chance of making contact with her, which is a foul.

When a defender commits to the interception she should run hard on to the ball, as though it was actually being passed to her. Don't lunge for it.

PRACTICE No. 1

In threes, with one ball, two feeders and one defender.

- The feeders stand opposite each other 2.5 metres (8 feet) apart.
- The defender positions herself either slightly behind or to the side of one of the feeders.
- As the feeders pass the ball back and forth, the defender needs to anticipate

when the pass is going to be released and then drive on an angle towards the feeder to try to intercept the ball from the receiver.

- Once successful, jog to the other feeder and try again.

DID YOU KNOW?

The top nine teams in Britain compete in an annual Superleague, with matches shown live on satellite TV. Team Bath were the Champions in 2009, winning all 16 matches.

PRACTICE No. 2

- The two players stand facing each other, about half a metre (2 feet) apart.
- Player A throws the ball up high or bounces it hard close to her body.
- Player B has to run all the way around player A before she retrieves the ball at the front of player A.
- Player B should aim to retrieve the ball on only one bounce or, if it has been tossed up high, no bounce.
- Have three goes, then swap roles.

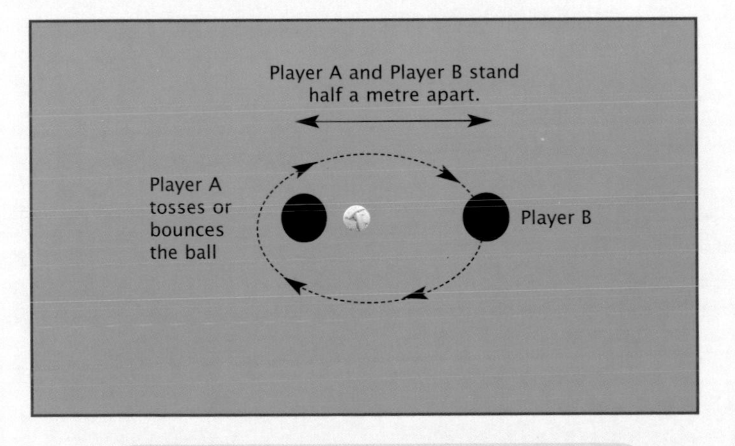

Practice No. 2: See how quickly you can run around player A before you catch the ball she has tossed or bounced.

Marking the pass or shot

When you are facing the player with the ball, you need to put pressure on to stop her passing it or shooting accurately. Remember, though, that when the attacker has the ball you must be at least three feet away from her first landing foot.

When you are marking the ball, try to angle your body so that you can see where the attacker intends to pass. Then you can either try to intercept the pass or block the vision of the attacker by making yourself as big as possible so that it is a real challenge for her to get around you.

If you can, mark the ball in lots of different ways:

1. Square-on with both arms, making yourself as big as possible.
2. By marking the attacker and then jumping when you think the ball is being released to intercept the ball.
3. On an angle, with one arm marking the side on which the ball is being held and then the other down by your side. Your 'hidden' hand then shoots out as the ball is being released.
4. On an angle with both arms out, slightly bent, so that the attacker can't anticipate how big your range is and you may be able to reach the pass with your fingertips.

It is similar when marking the shot, except the trajectory of the ball will be more like an upside-down 'J'. Therefore, in order to try and tip the shot, your hand needs to be high. Each shooter will release the ball at a different time, so try to work out their cue for shooting so that you can put on as much pressure as possible.

DID YOU KNOW?

The International Federation of Netball Associations (IFNA) is the internationally recognised governing body for netball.
There are 60 National Netball Associations affiliated to IFNA, grouped into five regions – Africa, Asia, Americas, Europe and Oceania. Each of these areas has its own Regional Federation.

Marking the pass: England's Ama Agbeze (right) tries to inhibit New Zealand player Maria Tutaia's pass during the New World International Netball Series 2008.

SHOOTING

Having accurate shooters with good technique is key to winning a game of netball, and the more you practise the better you will be. The best shooters can shoot from anywhere in the goal circle, so once you've mastered your technique...get practising!

PREPARATION

Although the shooter can't hold the ball for longer than three seconds, it is important to take your time when taking a shot at goal. The preparatory stance is crucial. Good balance helps accuracy, and that means a stable base.

Start with:

- Feet shoulder width apart and facing the post.
- Knees flexed.
- Back straight – trunk (above your hips and below your shoulders) held firmly.
- Arms slightly flexed.
- The ball resting comfortably in the palm and fingers of your dominant hand.
- The ball held high above and in line with, or slightly behind, your head.
- The non-shooting hand supporting the ball to the side.

The ball should rest comfortably in the palm and fingers of your shooting hand.

THE ACTION

- Bend your knees as if you are about to jump into the air. At the same time, bend your elbows down and back.
- As you shoot, straighten your legs and arms, but not to the point of them becoming stiff or locked.
- Release the ball as high as you can.
- Focus on a point at the back, rather than the front, of the ring and try to get the ball through the hoop without touching the sides.

- Move your arms as little as possible when you release the ball, but add spin by flicking your wrists.
- You should end your shot standing on tiptoes, with your hands following through towards the goal ring.

PRACTICE

Top international shooters practise daily, often shooting more than 200 goals at a time. So once you've mastered your technique through practice, try a few of these exercises.

1. Scatter cones around the shooting circle, or try putting them in a fan shape. See how many you can score out of three when standing next to each of the cones. Note how many you do score, so the next time you do it you can compare.
2. Practise taking a pass (either high, low, or to the side) from a partner or toss the ball to

Going for goal: 1. Line up in front of the goal post and get your body in the right position to make the shot.
2. Close up of body position.

yourself, doing the correct footwork (one-two). Then turn towards goal, set your shot and go for it! Try close-, middle- and long-range shots.

3. Start at the base line, next to the post. Sprint out to the edge of the circle and back again to the post, pick up the ball and shoot. Repeat, driving out on different angles. Do this ten times before you have a break. It's really important for a shooter to be able to shoot when they are tired!
4. If there are three of you, have one shooter, one defender, and one feeder. To begin with the defender marks the attacker, who has to get free in the circle to receive a pass from the feeder, and then turn to shoot. Once the attacker has done this a few times, the defender can add more pressure to stop the attacker getting free by marking the shot. If the attacker misses, practise going for the rebound.

3. Bend your knees to focus all your power into the shot.
4. Push up and shoot.